ANTS

Amy-Jane Beer

Grolier
an imprint of
SCHOLASTIC
www.scholastic.com/librarypublishing

Published 2008 by Grolier
An imprint of Scholastic Library Publishing
Old Sherman Turnpike, Danbury,
Connecticut 06816

For The Brown Reference Group plc
Project Editor: Jolyon Goddard
Copy-editors: Lesley Ellis, Lisa Hughes,
     Wendy Horobin
Picture Researcher: Clare Newman
Designers: Jeni Child, Lynne Ross,
     Sarah Williams
Managing Editor: Bridget Giles

Volume ISBN-13: 978-0-7172-6216-8
Volume ISBN-10: 0-7172-6216-2

**Library of Congress
Cataloging-in-Publication Data**

Nature's children. Set 1.
    p. cm.
  Includes index.
  ISBN-13: 978-0-7172-8080-3
  ISBN-10: 0-7172-8080-2
  1. Animals--Encyclopedias, Juvenile.
  QL49.N38 2007
  590--dc22

          2007018358

Printed and bound in China

PICTURE CREDITS

Front Cover: Shutterstock: Yaroslav

Back Cover: Nature PL: Kim Taylor;
Shutterstock: Tan Hung Meng; Superstock:
Age Fotostock.

Corbis: Martin Harvey 33, Layne Kennedy 9,
Karen Tweedy-Holmes 30, Jim Zuckerman
14; **FLPA**: Mark Moffett/Minden Pictures
26–27, 41; **Nature PL**: Phil Savoie 46;
Photos.com: 4, 29; **Shutterstock**: Raul A.
Alvarez 34, Tan Hung Meng 6, Mark William
Penny 5, 37, Johann Piber 18, Yaroslav 13, 17,
21; **Still Pictures**: BIOS/Chelle Herve 42,
Hecker 38, J. Kottmann 2–3, 22, J. Meul-Van
Cauteren 10, Gunter Ziesler 45.

Contents

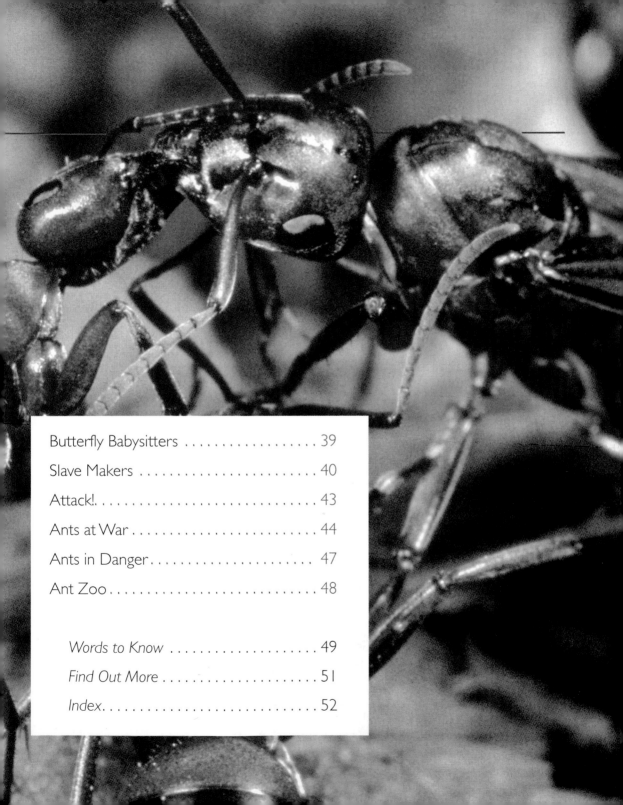

FACT FILE: Ants

Class	Insects (Insecta)
Order	Ants, bees, and wasps (Hymenoptera)
Family	Ants (Formicidae)
Genera	More than 280 genera worldwide
Species	About 12,000 species have been named
World distribution	Ants occur on all continents except Antarctica; they live in tropical and temperate areas
Habitat	Most ants live in woodlands or grasslands, but they explore all sorts of other places, including houses
Distinctive physical characteristics	An ant's body has three parts: head, thorax, and abdomen; there are six legs on the abdomen and two antennas on the head
Habits	Ants live in big family groups called colonies; they build nests and work together
Diet	Varied; different species eat leaves, fruit, meat, other insects, or fungi

Introduction

Who are the superheroes of the insect world?
Ants, of course! Ants are incredibly strong, have
super-senses, and never seem to give up. What's
more, every ant devotes its whole life to working
for the good of its **colony**. Ants have many skills
—they are outstanding engineers, bold explorers,
hard-working farmers, and fearless soldiers. Ants
work together to collect and produce food, look
after young, and defend the colony from attack.
In fact, humans could learn a lot from ants!

**An ant milks an
aphid for its sweet
honeydew.**

Ants build a bridge out of themselves if they have a gap to cross.

How Many Ants?

There are tens of thousands of different **species**, or types, of ants on Earth. At the last count, entomologists, or scientists who study insects, thought they had named about 12,000. But new types are being discovered all the time. In 2006, 89 new types of ants were discovered. And there are certainly more out there waiting to be found by sharp-eyed scientists.

These days scientists can use new technology to look closely at animals' genes. Genes control how an animal looks, develops, and breeds. They are passed on from parents to young. Genes help scientists tell how closely related different types of ants are. By looking at genes, scientists can tell if two ants belong to the same species.

Ant History

Ants have been around for a very long time—about 150 million years. Ants first appeared in the hot tropics. That is still where most types of ants live. The ancestor of all ants alive today was a kind of wasp. So wasps and ants are like cousins in the great family tree of life.

In the 1960s, a famous biologist named Edward O. Wilson was sent a piece of amber with a dead ant inside. Amber is ancient tree sap that has become solid. The ant was more than 80 million years old. It looked like a cross between a wasp and an ant. So Wilson named the ant *Sphecomyrma freyi* (SFEE-KOH-MUR-MA FRAY-I). *Sphecomyrma* means "wasp ant," and *freyi* comes from the name of the people (Frey) who sent the ant to Wilson. Since then, people have found many more *Sphecomyrma freyi* ants preserved in amber. If you go to a museum of natural history, you might see one for yourself.

This piece of amber contains a preserved winged ant that lived about 35 million years ago.

Winged black
ants land on the
tip of a leaf.

What Are Ants?

Ants are insects. Insects are small animals with six legs and three main parts to the body. The first part is the head, which has two **antennas**, or feelers. Next comes the **thorax**. That is where the legs attach. The last and largest part is the **abdomen**. Other types of insects include beetles, flies, and moths. The closest relatives of ants are wasps and bees.

Ants, wasps, and bees belong to a group of insects called the Hymenoptera (HI-MUH-NOP-TURRA). *Hymenoptera* means "membrane wings." A membrane is thin, skinlike tissue. Did you know ants sometimes have wings? The wings of all hymenopterans look a bit like old windows with lots of little panes of glass. In the wing of a wasp or flying ant, the panes are filled with a very delicate membrane, like plastic wrap.

Suit of Armor

We have already seen that ants are typical insects because they have a three-part body and six legs. Like other insects they also have a hard body covering called an **exoskeleton**. "Exo" means "outside." An exoskeleton is like the ant's skeleton. Ants do not have bones. The exoskeleton is a bit like a suit of armor that fits the ant's body perfectly. This special ant armor is made of a material called **chitin** (KI-TIN). As well as protecting the ant's insides, the exoskeleton also supports the body, doing much the same job as the skeleton of some larger animals.

Each of the ant's legs and both of its antennas have armor. Special joints allow the legs and antennas to move.

An ant's outer covering is made of a tough substance called chitin, which is a type of sugar!

13

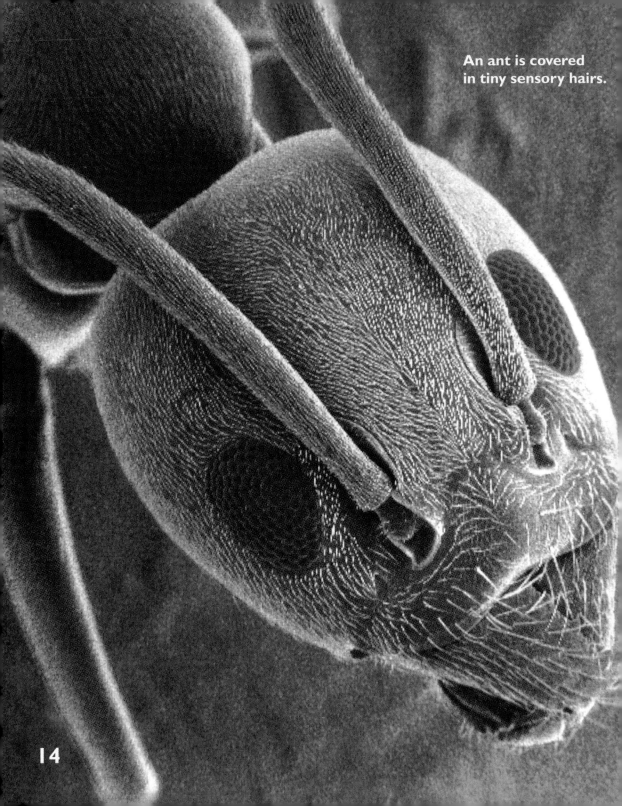

An ant is covered
in tiny sensory hairs.

14

Ant Senses

Ants have two large eyes on their head. They are called compound eyes. Each eye is made up of many small eyes. Ants certainly see the world very differently from people. While we see one picture, ants see dozens of little images. It must be confusing, but the ants are good at making sense of it all. Surprisingly, eyesight is not all that important to most ants. Some types of ants are even blind.

Most ants make up for their poor eyesight with another set of sense organs. On their head, ants have two antennas, or feelers. Those not only touch and feel the world but also smell and sense the tiniest of vibrations.

All over the body, there are tiny hairs sticking out through the exoskeleton. These hairs work like a cat's whiskers, helping the ant sense the world by touch.

Ant Insides

The brain is the main control center in most animals. Ants have a tiny brain in their head. There are small control centers in other parts of the body, too. Those help sort out all the information that comes from the eyes, the antennas, and the sensory hairs on the body. The small control centers also send signals along pathways called nerves. These signals make the rest of the body react.

Ants do not have proper blood or blood vessels like veins and arteries. Instead, their muscles and internal organs, such as the stomach, are bathed in insect blood called hemolymph (HEE-MUH-LIMF). Hemolymph carries vital chemicals around the insect's body.

Ants do not breathe using lungs. Instead they take air in through tiny holes in the sides of the body called spiracles. The spiracles are connected to tiny tubes that pass though the body. The tubes carry oxygen straight to the muscles and other parts of the body that need it.

An ant's brain
makes sense of
all the information
sent from the eyes,
antennas, and hairs.

Small claws on an ant's feet let it easily climb smooth surfaces.

Getting a Grip

Ants are amazing climbers. Vertical surfaces as smooth as glass are no problem for ants to scale. They can even walk upside down. If you watch an ant moving over a plant, you may see it walking on the underside of a leaf or up a stem just as easily as is does on the flat ground. How do ants do that without falling off?

The answer lies in their feet. At the tip of each of its six feet, an ant has tiny claws. The claws act like grappling hooks or a mountaineer's spiked boots. They latch on to the most minute cracks and bumps in any surface. With six sets of these claws, an ant can get a good grip on almost anything.

Slicing and Dicing

An ant's mouth is surrounded by an amazing set of tools. These mouthparts can act like built-in silverware. The mouthparts grip and chop food before it is eaten.

In different ants, the mouthparts may also do other things. Some parts are like shears for snipping up leaves. Other parts are used like saw blades or chisels to cut into wood. Some ants use their mouthparts as weapons. The mouthparts of some ants are large enough to give a person a nasty nip.

The jaws of an ant pack
a powerful bite that
can scare off or kill
unwelcome intruders.

Worker ants look after
a newly emerged queen.

Big Family

Ants live in groups called colonies. There are three types, or **castes**, of ants in a colony. First, there is a single very large female ant, called the queen. Most of the rest of the colony are small females, called workers. All the workers have the same mother, the queen. Because they are all sisters, the worker ants have a special bond.

Workers work hard all their lives, They build and look after the nest, collect food, and care for the queen and all the eggs and young she produces. A young ant is called a **larva**, or grub. It looks like a tiny, pale caterpillar. The third sort of ant in a colony is the males. They do not live long. Their only job is to **mate** with the queen.

Flight of Fancy

Toward the end of her life, the queen produces eggs that get very special treatment. The ants developing inside these eggs will not become workers but new queens and males. When the eggs hatch into grubs, they are given special food. That helps them grow large, develop wings, and be able to breed when they are adults. Before a grub becomes an adult, it produces a silky thread that it uses to make itself a covering called a **cocoon**. Inside the cocoon, the grub does not eat or move. This lifestage is called a **pupa**.

When the new queens and males eventually emerge from their cocoon, they form a big swarm. These new adults leave the nest and fly into the air. All the males drive themselves into a frenzy trying to mate with the queens. They mate in the air. After about an hour, the males drop to the ground and soon die. The young queens, however, are much stronger and they have a long life ahead of them.

Royal Duties

The main job of a queen ant is to start a new colony. After she has mated, a young queen must find a good place to build her nest. Soon after settling, her wings drop off. So, she spends the rest of her life in the same place.

To begin with, the queen has to work alone. She starts with a small nest just big enough for her and her first batch of eggs. She cares for the eggs herself. The queen cleans her eggs. When the grubs hatch from the eggs, she feeds them on a kind of saliva soup. This liquid is made by her own body tissues. After several months, a grub becomes a pupa. The pupae hatch into worker ants, which then take over a lot of the work. The queen is left with nothing to do but keep producing more eggs. Sometimes queens produce eggs for 10 or 15 years!

A fire ant queen is much bigger than her daughter workers. The workers look after and feed the white grubs.

Passing Messages

Communication is an essential part of keeping an ant colony running smoothly. Ants use chemical signals the way people use words and sentences —to pass information to one another. The special chemicals used for signaling are called **pheromones** (FER-RUH-MONES).

The queen ant produces the strongest pheromone signals of all. The pheromones that leak from her body are carried away by the workers that touch her. In no time, the signal has spread throughout the colony. Other ants use pheromones to signal that they have found food or that they sense danger. Grubs release hunger signals that encourage workers to feed them.

Two worker ants communicate by using their antennas to pass on special chemicals called pheromones.

Foraging ants form
a row on the way
to a source of food.

Ant Explorers

Worker ants spend a lot of time looking for food. You might see a lone ant busily scuttling along, maybe stopping from time to time to wave its antennas. The ant is probably a **scout** looking for food.

She's hoping to find something good, such as a shrub with tender new leaves, a flower with some tasty pollen, or maybe the bowl of sugar you left out in the kitchen. If successful, she rushes back to the nest and alerts the other ants. Soon a whole row of ants will be marching out to help bring the food back to the nest.

Which Way Now?

Ants have an amazing ability to find their way.
When they are marching as an army, it is easy
for each worker to follow the one in front. But
how does the first ant know where to go? And
how do scouts that spend hours wandering here
and there always seem to know the shortest
route home?

The answer is not a simple one. It seems ants
use lots of different methods for finding their
way. Ants clearly recognize certain landmarks.
So part of their skill is having a good memory
for directions such as, "Turn left at the toadstool"
or "Straight on over the broken twig." Ants also
use scent and the chemical trails of other ants.
But even without these clues, ants find their
way. Amazingly, they also use the Sun to find
their way home.

Army ants from Africa seem to know exactly where they are going when raiding for food.

Hungry insect-eating ants quickly eat any prey they come across when looking for food.

On the Menu

Ants eat all kinds of foods, from leaves to the sandwiches off your picnic plate. Some ants are vegetarian and eat mainly leaves, seeds, flowers, or nectar. Nectar is a sweet liquid made by some flowers. Certain ants catch and kill other insects. And some ants feed on the rotting remains of larger animals.

Worker ants do not eat all the food they find. They carry most of it back to the nest in a special stomach called the **crop**. Back at the nest, the ant brings the food back up from its crop to share with other ants. The queen is too busy producing eggs to find her own food. She relies on the workers to feed her and all the grubs. Often, the grubs cannot eat the food the adult workers collect. The workers have to prepare the food specially for the grubs. They mince up seeds into crumbs or soften leaves in their crop. The workers then cough it up as pulpy ant baby food.

Ant Farmers

While some ants are hunters and some are gatherers, others are farmers. Leaf-cutter ants snip up leaves and carry them back to the nest. A row of leaf-cutters looks like a tiny parade of marchers, waving green banners and placards. The leaf pieces weigh several times more then the ants themselves. Yet the ants carry the pieces easily. The leaves are not for eating. Back at the nest, the ants chew up the leaves and spit them out. That makes a mush, or compost. A type of living thing called a fungus grows on this compost. The ants eat this fungus and also feed it to their young.

Other ants farm livestock. **Aphids** are small insects that suck sap from plants. If an aphid is stroked in just the right way, it leaks a sweet juice called honeydew—a bit like milk from a cow. Ants "milk" aphids for honeydew. The aphids do not seem to mind. Also, being looked after by ants makes the aphids safer from predators such as ladybugs.

Ants "milk" aphids for a sweet liquid called honeydew.

37

The caterpillar
of the large blue
butterfly from
Europe lives in
ant nests. It gives
the ants honeydew
but also eats their
eggs and grubs.

38

Butterfly Babysitters

Ants are so good at caring for their young
that some other insects use their expert baby-
care service. A rare European butterfly called the
large blue lays its eggs on an herb called thyme.
Red ants collect the butterfly's caterpillars and
take them to their nest. There, the ants milk
the caterpillars for honeydew, just like the
aphids described earlier.

The caterpillar needs to eat, too. It seeks
out the ant grubs and eggs and eats them. The
caterpillar must pupate before it can become
a butterfly. The caterpillar spins a cocoon and
pupates in the ant nest. That is the time when
it is most likely to be killed by the ants. But the
pupa takes on a special ant scent and makes
noises like an ant grub about to hatch. If the
pupa survives, it turns into a butterfly and
leaves the nest.

Slave Makers

Some ants have a really sneaky way of making a living. They force types of ants to become slaves that do all the hard work. There are lots of different ways to make slaves. Often, it starts when a slave-maker queen enters a colony. She kills the rightful queen and gets the workers there to start taking care of her eggs. The slaves do not realize they are being used because the slave-maker queen produces chemicals very similar to those of the queen she killed.

The slave-maker queen lays eggs that hatch into more slave-maker workers. These workers go out and raid the nests of other ants. The slave-making ants bring back ants and grubs, which are made into more slaves when they hatch. Some slave-maker ants rely so much on slaves to do everything that without slaves they starve, even if surrounded by food!

A slave ant worker grooms
the slave-making queen.

If you accidentally step on an ant nest, you might get a nasty itch from ant bites or stings.

Attack!

Sooner or later, most people get bitten or stung by an ant. It could happen any time you are out in the backyard or countryside. Most times you won't even feel it. But you might get an itch later. Ants bite using their large mouthparts. Other ants, such as fire ants, have a stinger in the tail. They use the stinger to inject a burning chemical called **formic acid** into their enemy—ouch! The most serious ant attacks usually happen when someone accidentally steps on an ants' nest.

Wood ants use a different sort of chemical warfare. These ants produce a foul-smelling spray that sends most animals running in the opposite direction!

Ants at War

Most of the time, an ant's life is peaceful and well organized. But emergencies do occur, such as when the nest is attacked by a predator. Many animals eat ants, including anteaters, aardvarks, lizards, and birds. Insects, such as some beetles and even other ants, eat ants, too. When an ants' nest is attacked, the workers try to drive off the attacker.

The first workers to sense danger produce a powerful chemical signal. That is like a smellable emergency alarm! Instantly, other workers come pouring out of the nest. Sometimes, the cause of the alarm is clear: a hungry anteater or a raiding party of large killer ants. Other times, the ants just seem in the mood for a fight. They turn on one another. Perhaps they are practicing for a real emergency.

A giant anteater from Brazil sucks up ants or termites with its long snout.

Tropical ants, such as this giant ponerine ant, are under threat from the loss of their rain forest home.

Ants in Danger

Sadly, many ant species are in danger of becoming extinct, or dying out. Some species are already extinct. Conservationists are people who protect animals and plants and the places they live. These people fear that some ants might disappear before we even discover them. That is probably happening all the time in the tropics, where most species of ants live. There, people are destroying huge areas of forest by logging or burning to make way for farms or houses.

Ant Zoo

Did you know that zoos are not just for big animals like tigers and elephants? These days zoos are places that look after all kinds of wildlife, including ants. By breeding rare ants, some zoos around the world are doing an important conservation job. An ant zoo is called a **formicary**. It's the perfect place to go and watch these busy insects going about their daily lives.

You'll be able to see them harvesting food, repairing their nest and feeding the young. Some zoos and natural history museums even have webcams in their ant houses, so you can watch from the other side of the world.

Words to Know

Abdomen   The rear section of an insect's body.

Antennas   Feelers attached to an ant's head.

Aphids   Small insects that suck sap from plants.

Castes   Groupings of ants according to the job they do in the colony.

Chitin   Hard material that forms an ant's exoskeleton, or outer covering.

Cocoon   The covering for the ant pupa in which it develops into an adult ant.

Colony   A group of ants led by a queen.

Crop   Part of an ant's stomach. The crop stores food the ant can share later with other members of the colony.

Exoskeleton   Hard outer covering of an ant's body.

Formic acid   A stinging chemical made by ants.

Formicary   An ant zoo.

Larva   The second stage in an ant's life after it has hatched from an egg.

Mate   To come together to produce young.

Pheromones   Chemicals produced by an ant, usually the queen, that affect the behavior or development of other ants.

Pupa   The stage of an ant's life when it is inside a cocoon changing into an adult.

Scout   A worker ant that searches for food.

Species   The scientific word for animals of the same type that breed together.

Thorax   The middle section of an insect's body.

Find Out More

Books

Micucci, C. *The Life and Times of the Ant*. Boston, Massachusetts: Houghton Mifflin, 2006.

Squire, A. O. *Ants*. Danbury, Connecticut: Children's Press, 2004.

Web sites

Antcam
www.antcam.com
Watch an ant colony in action.

Ants
www.enchantedlearning.com/subjects/insects/ant/
Antcoloringpage.shtml
Facts about ants with a picture to print and color in.

Index